Love God Love Peoples

A Bible Study for the Curious

Dina L. Lieber

Love God, Love Peoples by Dina Lieber is a great booklet for people who are curious about the Christian faith, who are unfamiliar with the beliefs of Christianity or those who like to understand it better. It treats questioning people with respect and raises the questions many people have asked or wanted to ask. It is well written, easy to understand, and gently guides people to a serious examination of the Christian faith. I highly recommend this wonderful study!

Rev. Dr. Clark Cowden

Dina Lieber explains with simple, succinctly stated and historically documented facts why Christians believe in the truth of the bible… and the reality of Jesus Christ. A quick, compelling read, this book is a must for uninitiated seekers with lots of good questions!

Brian Morgan

Table of Contents

Prologue

I believe that God ministers to our hearts and minds through scripture, through fellowship, through meditation on Him, through giving us thoughts, ideas and even through dreams. I have not been a very good sleeper much of my adult life. My brain tends to become absorbed on problems, emotional pain, stresses or to-do lists. During one of my fitful nights, I became fixated on the phrase "Love God, Love Peoples." I realized that most people who are familiar with this fundamental Biblical principal do not pluralize "people," but my brain certainly would not let go of the idea. I recognized in my sleeplessness that "peoples" held a broader and inclusive meaning. It included not just the people I share my life with but people of all backgrounds, of all races and all nations. The political and social unrest that I had been witnessing in the media and in my own Chicago neighborhood over the past few years certainly left a mark on my soul. It pained me deeply to realize how intolerant our nation had become. From college campuses to violent street demonstrations, to politicians who choose to follow party lines rather than think for themselves, to a media culture that had become so unprofessional and biased that it was difficult to comprehend how our nation could heal its wounds with such vitriol against one another.

As God continued to work on my heart and mind in the days to follow, the idea of writing a scripture-based study guide on loving God and loving peoples worked its way onto my to-do list. It is my desire to share with people the truth of the Bible because it is a beautiful love story. I know that God dearly loves each of us and desires to have a personal relationship with us. Living in such a broken world, this idea may be confusing or perhaps unbelievable to you. It is not difficult to look around our society and realize that people are not at peace. The lack of peace and hope is spilling out in the form of disdain, disrespect, hatred, greed, selfishness, and even violence. If you are curious about how you can be at peace and have hope regardless of what this life throws your way, this study may help get you on the right path with God.

One of my favorite childhood stories is of the child by the seashore that is littered with beached starfish. The child picks up one starfish and throws it back into the sea and then another. With thousands of starfish scattered on the sand, the child's parent tells him that there are too many starfish for his efforts to matter. The child replies, "It matters to this one," as he throws it safely back into the water. With this study on loving God and loving peoples, I envision myself as the child on the beach seeking to share God's message of love even if it is only for one person that the message matters. I hope that person is you.

Lesson 1 - The Reliability of the Bible

Many people are blessed with the gift of faith. They innately know that the creator of the universe is speaking directly to them through the words of the Bible. I have met many Christians in my life's journey who "ooze" faith in God. They know scripture and their faith seems unshakeable. I, on the other hand, struggled as a teenager and into my early 20s with the idea of a loving God. I was not raised in a Christian home but my parents did not speak negatively about any religion. They gave me and my brothers the latitude to explore, or not explore, religions and decide for ourselves what to believe. My story of becoming a Christian did not revolve around extensive research into the scriptures. However, I have grown in my faith through the reading of God's word, being in fellowship with Christians and through reading books written about the scriptures as well as on Christian apologetics. I have been fascinated to learn that there have been numerous atheists over the generations who have sought to debunk scriptures only to be converted to Christianity because evidence of the life, ministry and resurrection of Jesus Christ are so compelling. C.S Lewis (1898-1963), Albert Henry Ross (1881-1950) and Lee Strobel (1952) are modern examples of highly-educated people who sought to prove that Christianity was a false religion only to become convinced of the divinity of Jesus Christ. By making their own deep dives into ancient records, they found overwhelming evidence that supports the historicity of the New Testament documents (Geisler & Bocchino 281).

I find the stories of people like C.S. Lewis and Lee Strobel captivating and their stories validate what I believe. However, sceptics may not be moved or take to heart the relevance of their testimonies. They may claim that a few converted men do not have impact on their belief systems or way of life. I want to be very clear on this point. The Bible claims that this man named Jesus lived, ministered, died on a cross, and then rose from the dead. It says that He appeared to over 500 people in a resurrected body. It says that He is the Son of God. If Jesus did not come back to life after being crucified, then nothing that is, or that Jesus said, in the Bible matters at all. But if it is true then your soul—your eternal life—is at stake. There is nothing more important than to determine whether this man Jesus was the real deal. No other religious figure has ever come back to life after dying. How do you know if He really came back to life? How do you know if He really even lived? To answer these questions, we will first take a look at the sources of information on the life of Jesus and examine their reliability.

In the book *Unshakeable Foundations* by Norman Geiser and Peter Bocchino, the authors test the reliability of the New Testament writings against criteria established by the military historian Dr. C. Sanders. Dr. Sanders' Bibliographical, Internal and External testing methods were developed to authenticate ancient documents. The Bibliographical Test determines how close and how numerous are the copies of texts when the original documents are no longer in existence. If the document is shown to be credible and truthful it passes the Internal Test. The External Test seeks other supportive material that validate the accuracy of the writings. Geiser and Bocchino are just two of many people throughout history who have gone to great effort to study the New Testament documents and apply these kinds of testing methods. Like others, Geiser and Bocchino conclude that "the New Testament is the most historically accurate and reliable document of all antiquity" and further state:

"If one cannot trust the New Testament at this point, then one must reject all of ancient history, which rests on much weaker evidence" (258).

The Bible comprises sixty-six books and is a diverse assemblage of writings over 1600 years by over forty authors (Comfort, 7). The Old Testament stories go back thousands of years and were communicated orally until written down many years later by Jewish prophets and scribes. The Old Testament is made up of thirty-nine books. The first five books are call the Pentateuch and there are twelve historical, five poetic and seventeen prophetic writings in the Old Testament. The New Testament is a composition of letters, memoirs and teachings from early Christians and were written in ancient Hebrew and Greek languages. There are over 5,600 Greek manuscripts of the New Testament in existence today (Geisler *et al.*, 256). Authenticating the wording of scripture there are over 24,000 Syrian, Latin, Aramaic and Coptic texts (Comfort, 64).

The number of New Testament manuscripts are far more numerous than the number of other ancient writings. For example, estimated to have been written around 900 B.C., there are 643 known copies of Homer's *The Iliad*. Although scholars seem to disagree on the authenticity of Plato's presumed writings, there are at least seven and at most 250 manuscripts attributed to him in existence today (Brumbaugh & Wells 73-75). At over 24,000, the number of New Testament manuscripts is extraordinary. Those who claim that Jesus was just a fable or that the stories about Him are fictional are unfamiliar with the facts. In addition to the number of New Testament writings by multiple authors, there are many ancient writings about the life of Jesus that exist outside of the New Testament. Author of more than forty books and co-host of the TV program "The Way of The Master" Ray Comfort from New Zealand writes: *"With the great body of manuscript evidence, it can be proved, beyond a doubt, that the New Testament says exactly the same things today as it originally did nearly 2,000 years ago...Critics also charge that there are no ancient writings about*

Jesus outside the New Testament. This is another ridiculous claim. Writings confirming His birth, ministry, death, and resurrection include Flavius Josephus (A.D. 93), the Babylonian Talmud (A.D. 70–200), Pliny the Younger's letter to the Emperor Trajan (approx. A.D. 100), the Annals of Tacitus (A.D. 115–117), Mara Bar Serapion (sometime after A.D. 73), and Suetonius' Life of Claudius and Life of Nero (A.D. 120)" (Fales & Comfort, 163). "*Over 25,000 archaeological finds demonstrate that the people, places, and events mentioned in the Bible are real and are accurately described. No archaeological finding has ever refuted the Bible. In fact, the descriptions in the Bible have often led archaeologists to amazing discoveries*" (Comfort, *How to Know,* 151).

Read the Bible passages below. Consider the messages being conveyed.

John 8:31-32. "So, Jesus said to the Jews who had believed in him, 'if you abide in My word, you are My disciples indeed. And you shall know the truth and the truth shall make you free.'"

Proverbs 30:5-6. "Every word of God is pure; He is a shield to those who put their trust in Him. Do not add to His words, Lest He rebuke you, and you be found a liar."

2 Timothy 3:16. "All Scripture is given by inspiration of God, and is profitable for doctrine, for reproof, for correction, for instruction in righteousness.."

Psalm 119:160. "The entirety of Your word is truth, and every one of Your righteous judgements endures forever."

Today, there are a wide variety of Bible translations available. Some of the best-known Bible versions include The King James Version (KJV), the Revised Standard Version (RSV) the New American Standard Version (NASB), The New International

Version (NIV) and the English Standard Version (ESV). Wycliff Bible translators report on their website that more than 1400 languages have access to the New Testament and more than 600 languages have the complete Bible translation. The original scripture texts are in Hebrew and Greek. Some translated Greek and/or Hebrew phrases and words do not match up exactly to the English language. What Bible scholars agree upon regardless of the English words selected is that the concept or idea is conveyed accurately in the translation. When compared to the Dead Sea Scrolls, "the King James Bible is 98.33 percent pure" (Geisler & Nix, 263). Discovered in the Judean Desert near the Dead Sea in 1946, The Dead Sea Scrolls include the second-oldest surviving Biblical manuscripts. As our English language has changed over the years, so too do the translations of the scripture that best convey the message of the original text. Some people like the melodic nature of the King James Version while others appreciate a more modern adaptation. *The Message (MSG)* by Eugene Peterson is modern-day adaptation that is very user-friendly. We often read multiple sources including *The Message* in our Bible study group that meets each week in our home in Chicago. Unless otherwise indicated, I quote from The New King James Bible. Any of the most common translations are acceptable in your Bible study voyage.

Bible version scripture comparisons for your review:

John 3:16 KJV: For God so loved the world, that he gave his only son that whosoever believeth in him should not perish but have everlasting life.

John 3:16 NIV: For God so loved the world, that he gave his one Son, that whoever believes in him should not perish, but have eternal life.

John 3:16 MSG: This is how much God loved the world: He gave his Son, his one and only Son. And this is why: so that no one need be destroyed; by believing in him, anyone can have a whole and lasting life.

Matthew 11:28 KJV: Come unto me, all ye that labour and are heavy laden and I will give you rest.

Matthew 11:28 NIV: Come to me, all you who are weary and burdened, and I will give you rest.

Matthew 11:28 MSG: Are you tired? Worm out? Burned out on religion? Come to me. Get away with me and you'll recover your life.

Psalm 62:1 KJV: Truly my soul waiteth upon God: from him cometh my salvation.

Psalm 62:1 NIV: Truly my soul finds rest in God; my salvation comes from him.

Psalm 62:1 MSG: God, the one and only-I'll wait as long as he says. Everything I need comes from him, so why not?

1 Peter 4:7 KJV: But the end of all things is at hand: be ye therefore sober, and watch unto prayer.

1 Peter 4:7 NIV: The end of all things is near. Therefore be alert and of sober mind so that you may pray.

1 Peter 4:7 MSG: Everything in the world is about to be wrapped up, so take nothing for granted. Stay wide-awake in prayer.

In American culture our lives are very fast paced and we have the expectation of instant gratification. Take a moment and remove yourself from this day and age. Consider what it might have been like in the time of Jesus with no computers, telephones, televisions, internet or cell phones. It was a very different era and people spent their time in very different ways than we do. Communicating significant events was done with great care to get the stories just right. People memorized the details of events word for word to be sure that the information that was being transferred was accurate. When more than one person recorded an event, there were slight differences because people differ on some points of importance as they receive the information. There are numerous stories in the New Testament told by more than one witness or author. These stories have slight differences but the main themes of the stories align completely. Historians use this kind of alignment to support the reliability of the story. Slight differences between authors that do not take away from the main theme and message actually help prove the authenticity of the words written.

What are your questions about the reliability of the Bible?

Do you believe that Jesus actually lived?

Who do you think He was?

Lesson 2 - Prophecies Fulfilled

One of many unique features of the Bible is the fact of fulfilled prophecies—not just a few fulfilled prophecies but hundreds of them. Bible scholars have identified over three hundred prophetic scriptures describing the Jewish Messiah in the Old Testament. It may be surprising for some to learn that The New Testament was written mostly by Jews and thousands of Jewish people witnessed the life and ministry of Jesus Christ. During Jesus's short ministry life, thousands of Jews were baptized in His name.

No other religious documents contain prophecies of actual events that became true hundreds of years later. Prophecies include that the Messiah would be born in Bethlehem, would come from the line of Abraham, and that He would be rejected by His own people. The prophet Isaiah wrote about the future Messiah in the early 8th century, over 700 years before the birth of Jesus. His prophesies included that the Messiah would speak in parables, that He would be called a Nazarene, He would be silent before His accusers and that He would be crucified with criminals. It is important to know that the dates of the scriptures have been authenticated by historians. Below are just a few of the prophecies that came true in Jesus. These alone are compelling enough to validate the Messiahship of Jesus Christ yet many more have been documented.

Prophecy	Approx. Year of Prophecy	Old Testament Scripture	New Testament Fulfillment
The Messiah would be born in Bethlehem	Micah lived in the 8th Century BC – 700 years before Christ	Micah 5:2	Matthew 2:1 Luke 2:4-6
The Messiah would be born of a virgin	Isaiah lived in the later part of the 8th Century BC – over 600 years before Christ	Isaiah 7:14	Matthew 1:22-23 Luke 1:26-31
The Messiah would be rejected by His own people	a. David lived in the 10th Century BC – over 900 years before Christ b. 8th Century BC	a. Psalm 69:8 (by David) b. Isaiah 53:3	John 1:11 John 7:5
The Messiah would be declared the Son of God	10th Century BC	Psalm 2:7 (by David)	Matthew 3:16-17
The Messiah would speak in parables	a. 10th Century BC b. 8th Century BC	a. Psalm 78:2-4 b. Isaiah 6:9-10	Matthew 13:10-15, 34-35
The Messiah would be falsely accused	10th Century BC	Psalm 35:11	Mark 14:57-58
The Messiah would pray for His enemies	10th Century BC	Psalm 109:4	Luke 23:34
The Messiah's hands and feet would be pierced	a. 10th Century BC b. Zechariah lived in the 6th Century BC – over 500 hundred years before Christ	a. Psalm 22:16 b. Zechariah 12:10	John 20:25-27

Isaiah 53:7-8

"He was oppressed and He was afflicted,

Yet He opened not His mouth;

He was led as a lamb to the slaughter,

And as a sheep before its shearers is silent,

So He opened not His mouth.

He was taken from prison and from judgment,

And who will declare His generation?

For He was cut off from the land of the living;

For the transgressions of My people He was stricken."

Isaiah 53 was written approximately 700 years before Jesus was born, yet the words accurately describe what happened to Him. In addition to prophesies about the Messiah, predictions about empires, politicians, and the state of Israel can be found in the Old Testament. In the book *When Skeptics Ask*, the author Norman Geisler examines a prophecy in the Old Testament that the city of Tyre "would be destroyed and its ruins cast into the sea" (Ezekiel 26:2). This prophecy was written between 587 and 586 BC. The city of Tyre was destroyed by Nebuchadnezzar yet the ruins were left on the land for 200 years. It wasn't until Alexander the Great attacked Tyre and forced the residents of the city to flee to a nearby island that the prophecy came to its full revelation. Alexander the Great had all of the debris thrown into the sea to build a pathway that would reach the island and its inhabitants (Geisler & Brooks, 198). Additionally, the prophet Nahum prophesied that Nineveh would be destroyed by fire: "There the fire will devour you; the sword will cut you down and, like grasshoppers, consume you…" (Nahum 3:15). In the 1800s, archaeologists found evidence of the fulfilled prophecy. In the book *100 Prophecies* by Ray Konig, he quotes the *Encyclopedia Britannica*, which reported on the archaeological find: "...Nineveh suffered a defeat from which it never recovered. Extensive traces of ash, representing the sack of the city by Babylonians, Scythians, and Medes in 612 BC, have been found in many parts of the Acropolis. After 612 BC the city ceased to be important..." These examples are just a few of the over 300 hundred fulfilled Bible prophecies. There are a great many resources from which to expand one's knowledge of the historical evidence. Here are a few to select from if you are curious:

1. *Archaeology and Bible History by Joseph Free*

2. *When Skeptics Ask by Norman Geisler and Ronald Brooks*

3. *The Evidence Bible: Irrefutable Evidence for the Thinking Mind by Ray Comfort*

Old Testament scholar Dr. Gleason Archer wrote, *"The Holy Bible is like no other book in all the world. It is the only book which represents itself as the written revelation of the one true God... demonstrating its divine authority by many infallible proofs"* (Gleason,15).

What are the odds that these prophecies could or would come true? We have evidence of when these prophecies were written and we have evidence of their fulfillment. I have asked a few very smart people to help me determine the odds of the prophecies in the Bible coming true. A professor of statistics appraised that the number is probably not calculable due to the infinite number of variables. Even if we defined a number of variables from which to perform a calculation, he claimed that the odds would be too incredible to comprehend. In the book *Science Speaks*, by Peter Stoner and Robert Newman, the authors shed light on the statistical improbability of just eight of the prophecies coming true, let alone over three hundred: *"Suppose that we take 10^{17} silver dollars and lay them on the face of Texas. They will cover all of the state two feet deep. Now mark one of these silver dollars and stir the whole mass thoroughly, all over the state. Blindfold a man and tell him that he can travel as far as he wishes, but he must pick up one silver dollar and say that this is the right one. What chance would he have of getting the right one? Just the same chance that the prophets would have had of writing these eight prophecies and having them all come true in any one man, from their day to the present time, providing they wrote using their own wisdom."*

As we have learned, many more than eight prophecies from the Old Testament came true in history and in Jesus Christ. God used prophets to foretell the coming of future events including the coming of the Messiah. He gave them specific details about what would happen. He did not use just one prophetic man, but many, so that we could rest in the evidence that the words are from God. What an amazing way for the God of creation to reveal His Word to us. Inspired by The Holy Spirit, His words are meant to be shared with all people of all generations so all can know the truth.

Jeremiah 28:9

"The prophet who prophesies of peace, when the work of the prophet comes to pass, then that prophet will be known as one whom the LORD has truly sent."

Old Testament Prophets and Messianic Prophecies

Passage (NKJV)	Scripture	Prophet	Approx. Years Written Before Christ
Psalm 22:16-18	For dogs have surrounded Me; The congregation of the wicked has enclosed Me. They pierced My hands and My feet; I can count all my bones. They look at me and stare at Me. They divide My garments among them. And for my clothing they cast lots.	David	1000
Psalm 69:8	I have become a stranger to my brothers, And an alien to my mother's children.	David	1000
Micah 5:2	But you, Bethlehem Ephrathah, Though you are little among the thousands of Judah, Yet out of you shall come forth to Me. The One to be Ruler in Israel, Whose goings forth are from Old, From everlasting.	Micah	700
Zechariah 11:12	Then I said to them, "If it is agreeable to you, give me my wages; and if not, refrain." So they weighed out for my wages thirty pieces of silver.	Zechariah	500
Deuteronomy 18:18	I will raise up for them a Prophet like you among their brethren, and will put My words in His mouth, and He shall speak to them all that I command Him.	Moses	1400

Lesson 3 - Apostles, Authors and Martyrs

There are twenty-seven books in the New Testament. It is believed that only eight men wrote these books. Six of the eight were eyewitnesses to the life, ministry, death and resurrection of Jesus Christ. They were Peter, John the son of Zebedee, Matthew, Mark, Jude and James. The remaining two authors, Luke and Paul, did not know Jesus before the resurrection. In this section of our study we will review a little bit about each of these eight men including how they knew Jesus, what they wrote about Him and how most of them died as a result of preaching salvation in Jesus Christ.

The first four books of the New Testament, Matthew, Mark, Luke and John, are called the Gospels. The Gospels are the recorded accounts of the life, ministry and death of Jesus. After the death of Jesus, Luke was deeply involved in the early Christian movement. He took great care to record the events directly from eyewitnesses on the teachings, miracles, death, and resurrection of Jesus Christ. Paul, one of the most prolific New Testament writers, had a life-changing experience with the resurrected Jesus. Imagine that! Paul had a supernatural experience with Jesus after His death on the cross. It was so compelling that it completely transformed him and he authored fourteen of the twenty-seven New Testament books.

Who are the writers of The New Testament?

1. Peter- Also known as Simon, son of Jonah and called Cephas ("rock") by Jesus. Peter was a fisherman and the brother of the Apostle Andrew. He was hot-tempered yet tender-hearted. Peter left his fishing business, family and home to follow Jesus. Jesus said in Matthew 16:16-19, "Upon this rock I will build my church, and the gates of Hell will not prevail against it." Peter was imprisoned by

Herod for preaching salvation through Jesus Christ. Peter is the author of 1 and 2 Peter in the New Testament.

Passages on the Apostle Peter (Simon):

Luke 5:10. "..and so also were James and John, the sons of Zebedee, who were partners with Simon. And Jesus said to Simon, 'Do not be afraid. From now on you will catch men.'"

Acts 5:29. "But Peter and the other apostles answered and said: 'We ought to obey God rather than men.'"

2. John-The son of Zebedee and son of Salome, John is described six times in the Book of John as "the disciple whom Jesus loved." John was one of the core group of disciples with Peter and his brother James. John was a partner with his father, brother James and with Peter in the fishing trade. Jesus called the brothers James and John the "Sons of Thunder." James, John and Peter are considered the pillars of the Jerusalem church. These three were chosen to witness Jesus's divinity upon a mountain top (Mark 9:2-8). John was described as bold in Acts 4:13. A healer and preacher of the gospel, John was exiled to the island of Patmos and was the only apostle to die of old age. John wrote the Gospel of John, 1, 2, and 3 John and Revelation.

Passages on the Apostle John:

John 13:23. "Now there was leaning on Jesus' bosom one of His disciples, whom Jesus loved."

Acts 8:14. "Now when the apostles who were at Jerusalem heard that Samaria had received the word of God, they sent Peter and John to them…"

3. Matthew- Also known as "Levi," Matthew was the son of Alphaeus. A tax collector in Galilee, he left the tax collecting trade to follow Jesus. Because of his profession, it is assumed that Mathew was well-educated and knew how to read and write. However, tax collectors were also known to be corrupt. The selection of Matthew by Jesus as an Apostle reflected the grace and forgiveness available to all sinners. Later a pastor of a church in Damascus, Matthew is the author of the Gospel of Matthew. It is interesting to note that Matthew records in Matthew 28:2-15 that the soldiers guarding Jesus's tomb were bribed to say that the followers of Jesus stole His body in order to hide the fact of the resurrection. As someone who was connected to the political world as a previous tax collector, Matthew had inside information on the lie that was circulated among the Jews.

Matthew 9:9. "As Jesus passed on from there, He saw a man named Matthew sitting at the tax office. And He said to him, 'Follow Me.' So he arose and followed Him."

Matthew 10:5-6. "these twelve Jesus sent out and commanded them, saying: 'Do not go into the way of the Gentiles, and do not enter a city of the Samaritans. But go rather to the lost sheep of the house of Israel."

4. Jude- Also known as Judas (but not Judas Iscariot the betrayer of Jesus). Jude was possibly a half-brother of Jesus and called himself, "a bond servant of Jesus Christ and brother of James" (Jude 1). There is not much known about this author of the Book of Jude in the New Testament. Warning of false teachers in the body of Christ, Jude 17 reminds the reader to "remember the words that were spoken before by the apostles of our Lord Jesus Christ."

5. Mark- Possibly recording the memoirs of Peter, Mark was a native of Jerusalem and traveled with Peter to Rome and later traveled with the Apostle Paul. Mark is believed to have been younger than the rest of the Apostles and he may have even seen and listened to Jesus as a teenager in Jerusalem. The great attention to detail of the events provides a sense of authenticity that could only come from the account of an eyewitness.

Among many more events, you will find in Mark:

- Mark 1:14. John the Baptist preaching the gospel of the Kingdom of God.

- Mark 5:21-43. Jesus heals a woman and raises a girl from the dead.

- Mark 8:1-10. Jesus feeds 4000 people.

- Mark 14 and 15. Jesus is arrested, condemned to death and crucified.

- Mark 16:1-8. Jesus rises from the dead.

6. James the Brother of Jesus- Also known as *James the Just*, he was not one of the twelve Apostles. There is no record of James following Jesus during Jesus' life on Earth. Scriptures do record that James was skeptical about his brother's claims to be the Son of God until he met the resurrected Christ (1 Corinthians 15:7). James was well-versed in Jewish law and became known for his leadership of the Jerusalem church until he was killed for publically proclaiming that Jesus was the Son of God. James the Just was the writer of the book of James.

Some well-known passages from the Book of James:

James 1:2. "My brethren, count it all joy when you fall into various trials…"

James 1:22. "Be doers of the word, and not hearers only, deceiving yourselves."

James 5:16. "Confess your trespasses to one another, and pray for one another, that you may be healed. The effective, fervent prayer of a righteous man avails much."

7. Luke- Well-educated and acquainted with Roman culture, Luke left his position as a physician to travel with Paul after learning about the resurrected Jesus Christ. Luke was possibly the only gentile writer of the New Testament and did not know Jesus personally. He had the opportunity to talk with and record the stories of many sources of the time as well as with the Apostles. Luke writes careful historical accounts of eyewitness testimonies of the events and words spoken by the Lord Jesus Christ. His writings encompass nearly one-fourth of the New Testament in the combination of the Gospel of Luke and the Book of Acts.

Examples of Luke's historical accounts of the words of Jesus Christ:

Luke 9:55-56. "But He turned and rebuked them, and said, 'You do not know what manner of spirit you are of. For the Son of Man did not come to destroy men's lives but to save them…'"

Luke 12:22-23. "Then He said to His disciples, 'Therefore I say to you, do not worry about your life, what you will eat; nor about the body, what you will put on. Life is more than food, and the body is more than clothing.'"

8. Paul- Born in Tarsus near the southern coast of what is now known as Turkey, Saul was Jewish, a Roman citizen and a Pharisee (a strict observer of traditional Jewish law). Saul was a highly-educated Jewish zealot and "on-fire" for God. He believed deeply that Jewish law had to be followed to the letter and anyone who did not follow it was a blasphemer deserving incarceration or death. Saul believed that he was fighting to protect the name of the "one true God" and was very hostile toward the early Christians who he viewed as heretical. It is recorded in Acts by Luke that Saul entered houses and dragged men and women to prison (Acts 8:3) as well as threatened to kill those proclaiming Jesus as Lord. The pre-Christian Saul was on his way to Damascus to capture and accuse Christians when the resurrected Jesus appeared to him (Acts 9:3). Overwhelmed by God's glory, Saul fell to the ground. Jesus said to him, "Saul, Saul, why are you persecuting me?" Saul replied, "Who are you Lord?" and Jesus answered, "I am Jesus, whom you are persecuting" Acts 9:5. It was at that moment that Saul learned that the one true God is Jesus.

Renamed Paul, he was completely transformed and began teaching the Gospel of Christ to Jews and gentiles. The apostle Paul's signature salutation in his letters includes, "Grace to you and peace from God our Father and the Lord Jesus Christ." It is interesting to note that "Grace to you" was similar to the standard Greek greeting of the time. Shalom or "peace" was a typical Jewish blessing. By introducing the two salutations together, Paul sent a message to the recipients of the letters that both gentile and Jews are one in Christ. This was a revolutionary idea to both peoples, especially coming from Paul. Paul is a perfect example of how someone with the best education and what they think are the best intentions of serving God can be wrong. Yet God used Paul to deliver His gospel and we can read of Paul's devotion to spreading the love of Christ within the New Testament.

Passages on Saul after seeing the risen Lord:

Acts 9:9. "And he was three days without sight, and neither ate nor drank."

Acts 9:15. "But the Lord said to him, 'Go, for he is a chosen vessel of Mine to bear My name before Gentiles, kings, and the children of Israel.'"

Acts 9:23. "Now after many days were past, the Jews plotted to kill him."

Other than John, all of the original Apostles died violent deaths at the hands of unbelievers because they would not renounce Jesus Christ as Lord of all. John was the last living disciple and the only Apostle to die of old age. Study the chart below and ponder for a few moments the fact that all of these Apostles of Christ died violent deaths because of their unwavering faith in Jesus Christ. Jesus had already died and they continued to preach the gospel of his saving grace. Why would the Apostles be willing to die cruel deaths rather than just renounce their belief? As they knew their brothers in Christ were being killed for preaching the gospel, why did they not just disappear into the background and go back to their original careers and lives?

What do you think caused the Apostles and disciples to have complete confidence in the truth of their message?

Name	Occupation	New Testament Books	Martyred
Peter – son of John	Fisherman, (Apostle)	I Peter, II Peter	By Crucifixion-upside down
James – son of Zebedee	Fisherman, (Apostle)		Beheading by King Herod
John – son of Zebedee	Fisherman, (Apostle)	John, I John, II John, III John, Revelations	NA: Old Age
Andrew – brother of Simon Peter	Fisherman, (Apostle)		Stoned and Crucified on X shaped cross
James – son of Alpheus	Unknown, (Apostle)		Unknown if Martyred
Thomas	Unknown, (Apostle)		By Sword
Philip	Unknown, (Apostle)		Unknown Method
Matthew	Tax Collector, (Apostle)	Matthew	By Sword or Spear
Bartholomew	Unknown, (Apostle)		Unknown. Possibly Flayed Alive
Simon the Zealot	Possibly a Politician, (Apostle)		Crucifixion
Thaddaeus	Unknown, (Apostle)		Unknown Method
Judas – son of Simon Iscariot	Unknown, (Apostle)		NA: Suicide by Hanging
Matthias – chosen to replace Judas	Unknown		Burning
Luke	Physician and fellow worker with Paul	Luke, Acts	Unknown if Martyred
James – Half-brother of Jesus	Possibly a Carpenter Later a pastor	James	Stoned or Clubbed
Paul – A murderer and persecutor of Christians but was transformed by a personal experience of the risen Christ	Jewish Pharisee (Post Resurrection Apostle)	Romans, Philippians, I Timothy, II Timothy, I Corinthians, II Corinthians, Colossians, Titus, I Thessalonians, II Thessalonians, Philemon, Galatians, Ephesians, Hebrews	Beheaded
Jude – Half-brother of Jesus	Possibly a Carpenter	Jude	Unknown if Martyred
Mark – Associate of Peter and Paul		Mark	Unknown if Martyred

Lesson 4 - The Resurrection

There is nothing more central or more significant to the Christian faith than the claim of the resurrected Jesus Christ. Without it, everything else in the faith falls apart. There is a significant amount of research available to anyone who is curious and many historians over the past 2000 years have written about the findings of their research on the matter. Many have commenced their research with the intent of proving that the resurrection was a lie. All have failed. Historian and Chair of Classics at Auckland University Professor E.M. Blaiklock (1903 -1983) wrote, *"I claim to be an historian. My approach to Classics is historical. And I tell you that the evidence or the life, the death and the resurrection of Christ is better authenticated than most of the facts of ancient history..."* (Hutchinson 51). Before Jesus was crucified, He told His disciples that He would die and three days later rise again. "Jesus answered and said to them, 'Destroy this temple, and in three days I will raise it up.' Then the Jews said, 'It has taken forty-six years to build this temple, and will You raise it up in three days?' But He was speaking of the temple of His body. Therefore, when He had risen from the dead, His disciples remembered that He had said this to them; and they believed the Scripture and the word which Jesus had said" (John 2:19-22).

The resurrection story is very compelling when taking into account the records of His appearances after His death. Matthew, Mark, Luke, John and Paul report that Jesus died, was buried, was raised from the dead and appeared to people after His resurrection. Paul reports in 1 Corinthians 15 that Christ appeared to Cephas (also known as Peter) to the apostles and to more than 500 of the brothers and sisters at the same time.

Open a Bible and read the below accounts of The Risen Christ:

Matthew 28

Mark 16

Luke 24

The resurrection of Jesus is a miracle. One of Jesus' disciples had a hard time believing it until he had an up-close-and-personal experience with the resurrected Christ. John 20:24-31 tells the story: "Now Thomas, called the Twin, one of the twelve, was not with them when Jesus came. The other disciples therefore said to him, 'We have seen the Lord.' So, he said to them, 'Unless I see in His hands the print of the nails, and put my finger into the print of the nails, and put my hand into His side, I will not believe.' And after eight days His disciples were again inside, and Thomas with them. Jesus came, the doors being shut, and stood in the midst, and said, 'Peace to you!' Then He said to Thomas, 'Reach your finger here, and look at My hands; and reach your hand here, and put it into My side. Do not be unbelieving, but believing.'"

Critics claim that the disciples stole the body of Jesus after His body was placed in the tomb. However, in review of the events leading up to and following the death of Jesus that scenario is highly unlikely. Recorded in the Bible and validated by historians, it was the burial custom to wrap a deceased body with a 100-pound mix of substances and aromatic spices bound with strips of linen (John 19:39-40). Bodies were placed in caves and closed with a solid rock using giant levers. With careful review of the scriptures, it can be estimated that there were at least four guards at Jesus' tomb. Matthew 19:23 says that there were four soldiers at the crucifixion of Jesus. The Pharisees petitioned Pilate for a guard (a guard is likely a squad of soldiers) at the burial tomb because they feared that the disciples would try to steal the body (Matthew 27:64). Roman guards affixed seals on tombs so as to prevent vandalism (Matthew 27:66). The consequences of breaking the Roman seal on a tomb meant execution by the perpetrator as well as the assigned the Roman guards. The threat of failure by the Roman guards was severe and could include being burned alive. Thus, they were highly motivated to be certain that no one moved the stone and stole the body. The fact that the area was teeming with pilgrims and followers of Jesus during the Passover, combined with the level of concern that Pilate and the Pharisees had over the possibility of the body of Jesus being stolen, make it likely that the number of soldiers at the tomb was sizeable. The very unlikely situation of all the soldiers falling asleep at the same time allowing the disciples to steal the body is not plausible even from the most ardent arguers against the resurrection. The noise and effort needed to remove the stone from the cave and carry away the heavily dressed body without waking at least one soldier is virtually impossible to believe.

What happens in the days that follow is spectacular. The resurrected Jesus appeared to His Apostles and disciples including 500 witnesses (1 Corinthians 15:3-8) over a forty-day period. The disciples, who had once hidden in fear of suffering the same fate as Jesus (Matthew 26:58, Mark 14:54, Luke 22:54), became empowered by the Holy Spirit and acted with new zeal and fervor. Speaking boldly about the saving grace of Jesus Christ, they spread the message of the resurrected Christ near and far. This transformation should not be skimmed over lightly. In the face of persecution and likely death, the disciples of Jesus did not waver in delivering their message. Not one backed down and left the cause. Not one renounced their faith in Jesus to save themselves.

Mark and Luke recorded the final discussion with His disciples before Jesus was taken up to heaven. Jesus gave the disciples what is known as "The Great Commission." As recorded in Luke 24:45-49, the gift of the Holy Spirit to guide and comfort believers was given not long thereafter.

Matthew 28:19-20. "The Great Commission."

"Go therefore and make disciples of all the nations, baptizing them in the name of the Father and of the Son and of the Holy Spirit, teaching them to observe all things that I have commanded you; and lo, I am with you always, even to the end of the age. Amen."

Acts 2:1-8

"When the Day of Pentecost had fully come, they were all with one accord in one place. And suddenly there came a sound from heaven, as of a rushing mighty wind, and it filled the whole house where they were sitting. Then there appeared to them divided tongues, as of fire, and one sat upon each of them. And they were all filled with the Holy Spirit and began to speak with other tongues, as the Spirit gave them utterance. And there were dwelling in Jerusalem Jews, devout men, from every nation under heaven. And when this sound occurred, the multitude came together, and were confused, because everyone heard them speak in his own language. Then they were all amazed and marveled, saying to one another, 'Look, are not all these who speak Galileans? And how is it that we hear, each in our own language in which we were born?'"

What do you think being "Filled with the Holy Spirit" is about?

Why do you think that the disciples of Jesus were able to speak in foreign languages?

Do you believe that God is with you always?

Lesson 5 - The Shedding of Blood

Sin is a big deal to God. A Holy God cannot be in the presence of sin and, as sinful people, we need a way to be forgiven if we are to be in His presence. We learn in the Old Testament that God provided a sacrificial system for the Jewish people. When a man sinned, he was able to ask for forgiveness and provided an animal to be sacrificed (judged) for the sin as a substitute for the man himself. It was only through the shedding of the animal's blood and the asking of forgiveness that God could stay in communion with His people. Hebrews 9:22 says that "without the shedding of blood there is no forgiveness." The taking of the animal's life was to be watched, felt and witnessed by the sinner to remind him that there is a price to pay and there are consequences for sinning. "Sin causes death" was the message and the lesson taught by the sacrificial system. In this law, the animal was the sinner's proxy and God allowed the substitution because He loves us and wants us to be in fellowship with Him.

Passages on sacrifices from the Old Testament:

Exodus 29:10-14. "You shall also have the bull brought before the tabernacle of meeting, and Aaron and his sons shall put their hands on the head of the bull. Then you shall kill the bull before the Lord, by the door of the tabernacle of meeting. You shall take some of the blood of the bull and put it on the horns of the altar with your finger, and pour all the blood beside the base of the altar. And you shall take all the fat that covers the entrails, the fatty lobe attached to the liver, and the two kidneys and the fat that is on them, and burn them on the altar. But the flesh of the bull, with its skin and its offal, you shall burn with fire outside the camp. It is a sin offering."

Leviticus 17:11. "For the life of the flesh is in the blood, and I have given it to you upon the altar to make atonement for your souls; for it is the blood that makes atonement for the soul."

Numbers 6:14. "And he shall present his offering to the Lord: one male lamb in its first year without blemish as a burnt offering, one ewe lamb in its first year without blemish as a sin offering, one ram without blemish as a peace offering..."

When Jesus arrived on the scene, John announced Him in John 1:29 saying, "Behold, the Lamb of God, who takes away the sins of the world!" Jesus came to break the chains of sin for Jews and gentiles. He was the once-and-for-all sacrifice for our sins. Because of Jesus, we no longer need to shed an animal's blood seeking forgiveness for our sins. The shedding of Christ's blood, His suffering and His death fulfill Old Testament scriptures of a Messiah who would come and save the world. We are saved by His life (Romans 5:10). Our sins are washed away and we are presentable to the Holy God of all creation.

If Jesus is God, why would He allow himself the torture of floggings, beatings, betrayal and being nailed to a cross? He chose to do it because of His love for us. It is a love story with Christ as the bridge between our fallen and sinful nature and the righteousness, purity and holiness of God the Father. Jesus was not simply a man who was born 2000 years ago. He is all-powerful, sovereign, all-knowing, pure and perfect. We are not. He is God in the flesh. He, the Father and the Holy Spirit are one. They are in community with one another at all times with each providing us a glimpse of the character of God. Known as The Trinity, the Father, Son and Holy Spirit work together in all things including creating our world. "In the beginning was the Word and the Word was with God, and the

Word was God. He was in the beginning with God. All things were made through Him and without Him nothing was made that was made. In Him was life and life was the light of men. And the light shines in the darkness and the darkness did not comprehend it" (John 1:1-5).

Yet, on the cross, Jesus was disconnected from the love of the Father as He took all the sins of the world upon Himself. He knew from the beginning of creation that He would have to enter into our lowly world so that a connecting bridge between us and God could be established for all time. The moment Jesus died, the entire story changed for mankind. Sin still causes death but when we accept Jesus as our surrogate, God sees us through the lens of Jesus Christ. Jesus is the airbrush and the "Photoshop" we so desperately need to be in the presence of a Holy God. To accept Jesus means that we accept the gift of a free makeover allowing Him to create in us a new person, a new vision and a new path in our lives. This seems so simple, yet so hard to comprehend.

In John 1:5 we are told that "the darkness did not comprehend the light of men." Jesus is the light of men and many who met Jesus while He physically walked the earth rejected Him because they did not understand or believe Him. "For God did not send His Son into the world to condemn the world, but that the world through Him might be saved" (John 3:17).

I think that some people believe that being a Christian means judging others and excluding them. That is not the message of Christ. He welcomes all people to be in relationship with Him. He took on all the sins of the world of every generation upon that cross so that all can be free and have hope for eternal life. The burden, pain and suffering that He felt is something that our minds cannot comprehend. It certainly isn't something that a mere mortal man could take on.

I envision that, in my acceptance of the shedding of Christ's blood for my sins, a beautiful white blanket washes over me and that I am made clean and pure and prepared to be in the presence of a Holy God. This new perfected state of my body and soul gives me direct access to God the Father. I don't need anything or anyone else to be in communion with God.

Isaiah 64:8

"But now, O Lord,

You are our Father;

We are the clay, and You our potter;

And we are the work of Your hand."

What does it mean to you to be "saved"?

Lesson 6 - The Holy Spirit Inspired Word

God designed us with freewill. He wants us to freely choose Him as Lord of our lives. We choose to follow Him or not. We choose to trust and to have faith. I like to think that it is a little like agreeing to an arranged marriage. The couple takes a huge step of faith and they trust the discernment of others in the match. In some cases, the bride and groom meet for the first time on the day of the wedding. Yet before the wedding day, it is expected that they freely commit themselves to each other. They choose to be in a committed relationship with a stranger. In ideal situations, that commitment turns into a deep love that can last a lifetime. God is asking us to take a step of faith in choosing Him. Yet, he has given us a love letter in the form of the Holy Spirit inspired Bible so that we do not have to choose blindly but with our eyes and hearts wide open. When we accept the "marriage" between ourselves and Jesus, we begin the journey that leads to a deep love. The Holy scriptures in the Bible guide and lead us, giving us the food our spirits need to deal with every aspect of our lives. "For the word of God is living and powerful, and sharper than any two-edged sword, piercing even to the division of soul and spirit, and of joints and marrow, and is a discerner of the thoughts and intents of the heart" (Hebrews 4:12).

Because the writing of scripture was not done by man alone but by men moved by the Holy Spirit, it comes alive and active in ways that cannot be humanly explained. With daily study, prayer and meditation on God's Word, you are opening the door of your heart and allowing the Holy Spirit to speak to you directly. As you learn about His plan for humanity and for you personally, it becomes easier to put your trust in the Lord, let go of the controls, and allow Him to direct your path. The one-time popular bumper stickers that said, "God Is My Co-pilot," were well-intentioned but missed the mark. "God Is My Pilot," is the goal whereby we submit everything to Him in prayer and supplication. It is because His Word is living and powerful that we can rest in it, allow it to transform our hearts and minds and give us hope and peace even in our most difficult times.

Reflect on these scriptures:

1 Corinthians 2:13. "…the Holy Spirit is the teacher of the wisdom of God."

2 Peter 1:20-21. "But know this first of all, that no prophecy of Scripture is a matter of one's own interpretation, for no prophecy was ever made by an act of human will, but men moved by the Holy Spirit spoke from God."

Zechariah 7:12. "The Lord of hosts had sent by His Spirit through the former prophets."

Ephesians 3:4-5. "By referring to this, when you read you can understand my insight into the mystery of Christ, which in other generations was not made known to the sons of men, as it has now been revealed to His holy apostles and prophets in the Spirit."

Scriptures that speak of the Holy Spirit inspired Word of God:

John 14:26. "But the Helper, the Holy Spirit, whom the Father will send in My name, He will teach you all things, and bring to your remembrance all things I said to you."

John 3:34. "For He whom God has sent speaks the words of God, for God does not give the Spirit by measure."

Acts 1:8. "But you shall receive power when the Holy Spirit has come upon you; and you shall be witnesses to Me in Jerusalem, and in Judea and Samaria, and to the end of the earth."

Acts 1:16. "Men and brethren, this Scripture had to be fulfilled, which the Holy Spirit spoke before by the mouth of David concerning Judas, who became a guide to those who arrested Jesus;"

2 Timothy 3:16. "All scripture is given by inspiration of God, and is profitable for doctrine, for reproof, for correction, for instruction in righteousness…"

Romans 8: 2-6

"For the law of the Spirit of life in Christ Jesus has made me free from the law of sin and death. For what the law could not do in that it was weak through the flesh, God did by sending His own Son in the likeness of sinful flesh, on account of sin: He condemned sin in the flesh, that the righteous requirement of the law might be fulfilled in us who do not walk according to the flesh but according to the Spirit. For those who live according to the flesh set their minds on the things of the flesh, but those who live according to the Spirit, the things of the Spirit. For to be carnally minded is death, but to be spiritually minded is life and peace."

Who is the author of Romans?

To whom was the book of Romans written?

What does Romans 8:2-6 mean to you?

Lesson 7 - The Grace of God

A very long time ago, I was taking a debate class at Chaffey College in Rancho Cucamonga, California. Yes, there really is a place called Rancho Cucamonga. The assignment was to offer a topic to the class and see if anyone was willing to debate you on the subject. I was not in a good place with God at the time and was angry with Him. I had been deeply hurt by the treatment I received from Christian teenagers during a high school youth group experience. My response was to reject them and reject God. The topic I offered up to the class was "Religion is a Joke." I was pro the topic and sought a con debater. The class was a little shocked at my topic and I did not care. A young and gentle Christian lady offered to take me on. I was on a mission to crush her every word. The sad thing is that I succeeded. I was more prepared, angry and determined than she was. She quoted Bible scriptures in her defense but really was not equipped to answer my direct and hard questions. The class had no option but to name me the "winner" of the debate. As I walked out of the classroom, my smugness disappeared and I felt a dark shadow overcome me. I felt sick and sad and almost as if the God of the Universe was grieved. I will never forget that day or that feeling of loneliness. I had a taste of what it felt like to be outside of God's grace and His protection. It was not good. We are taught in scripture that those who reject Jesus will live in eternity outside the presence of God. I was taught a very important lesson in my debate experience—I did not want to be alone and without God.

It was not long after that debate experience that my mother was diagnosed with cancer. My life was rocked to its core. I had accepted Christ as my Savior when I was five years old. Even though I believe that I saddened God with my anger toward Him, He waited patiently for me to return. And I did. Praise God! I was at the lowest point of my young adult life and was experiencing physical pain from the depths of my heartbreak. I opened myself up and asked God to reveal Himself to me. If He truly was the God of Abraham, Isaac and Jacob then I wanted Him to show me. God met me in a very personal way when I needed it most. He gave me strength and courage and peace. The Holy Spirit comforted me and I have clear memories of when and how God met me in my pain and transformed my heart and my mind. Through this experience, I learned a very important lesson about faith. Faith is not having all the answers. Faith is not trusting only in my own mental devices. I came to the realization that, in my earthly body, I do not and will not have the answers that the world wants to hear. I do know that God is God and He created the world and He is the decider of the rules, not me and not you. I have a God story and He transformed me. One of the ways that God continues to renew my faith is through fellow believers. Their transformation stories are amazing and enforce the mystery of a God who knows us uniquely and loves us deeply. "And be not conformed to the world, but be transformed by the renewing of your mind, that you may prove what is the good, and acceptable and perfect will of God" (Romans 12:2).

With all this magic and mystery of faith in Christ, it is unbelievably difficult for some people to move past the idea that Jesus Christ is the only way to heaven. "I am the way, the truth, and the life. No one comes to the Father except through Me" (John 14:6). It is not uncommon to hear people seeking the truth asking how a loving God whom claims to be full of grace and mercy only allows followers of Jesus Christ into eternity. There are those who believe that they are "good people" and give of their time and treasure in generous service of others. They may believe by doing good works and being a good person that a loving God will provide them access to eternity in heaven. Yet, according to scripture, being a good person does not "perfect" you and allow you to be in the presence of a Holy God. I think that we, especially in western cultures, do not truly comprehend the absoluteness and majesty of a Holy God. Our culture's focus on personal "rights" and what the world owes us for just existing (jobs, health care, safe spaces) does not leave room for the truth of our lowliness and God's sovereignty and pure holiness. Being good enough is not the goal nor the plan according to scripture. Accepting the free gift of salvation through Christ Jesus and living a Christ-centered life is the design. It is through God's grace that "He gave his only begotten son that whosoever believes in Him shall not perish but have eternal life" (John 3:16). It is God's choice to gift us with His unmerited favor. There is nothing we can do to earn God's grace. It is a free gift available to anyone who accepts it in the form of believing in His Son.

God knows our humanness and weaknesses. He knows that we fall short on a daily basis. One of the arguments against Christianity is that believers can continue to sin including adultery, lying, stealing and more without penalty because as long as Christians are saved by God's grace, they have eternal life. Our actions and obedience to His Word and our walk with God demonstrate the true condition of our hearts and belief in His promises. Does that mean that Christians are perfect and never sin? No! But there are consequences to sin. The Christian journey is replete with trials and tests of faith and we do not always make the right decisions. God uses our weakness and failings to grow and mature in a process called sanctification—to become more and more like Christ. If we are not diligently working toward becoming more and more like Christ in our love, forgiveness and grace (loving God and loving peoples) then the authenticity of the salvation event may be in question. As recorded in John 5 and John 8, Jesus warns two different people to go and "sin no more." He does not want us to return to sinful lifestyles and lose out on the transforming power of His grace and mercy. A sincere salvation event cannot be undone. However, there is much to lose and much at risk for continuing on a destructive path of sin. As a parent disciplines a child for doing wrong, so the children of God must face the consequences of a loving Father for their sins. He is always ready to forgive when we come to Him in prayer with a sincere desire to turn away from our sin. By shifting away from those things in our lives that cause us to stumble, God's grace is limitless. His grace fills us and gives us hope for a better day, not to mention eternity in His presence.

Read of God's Grace in John:

John 5:1-15. "After this there was a feast of the Jews, and Jesus went up to Jerusalem. Now there is in Jerusalem by the Sheep *Gate* a pool, which is called in Hebrew, Bethesda, having five porches. In these lay a great multitude of sick people, blind, lame, paralyzed, waiting for the moving of the water. For an angel went down at a certain time into the pool and stirred up the water; then whoever stepped in first, after the stirring of the water, was made well of whatever disease he had. Now a certain man was there who had an infirmity thirty-eight years. When Jesus saw him lying there, and knew that he already had been in that condition a long time, He said to him, "Do you want to be made well?" The sick man answered Him, "Sir, I have no man to put me into the pool when the water is stirred up; but while I am coming, another steps down before me." Jesus said to him, "Rise, take up your bed and walk." And immediately the man was made well, took up his bed, and walked. And that day was the Sabbath. The Jews therefore said to him who was cured, "It is the Sabbath; it is not lawful for you to carry your bed." He answered them, "He who made me well said to me, 'Take up your bed and walk.'" Then they asked him, "Who is the Man who said to you, 'Take up your bed and walk'?" But the one who was healed did not know who it was, for Jesus had withdrawn, a multitude being in that place. Afterward Jesus found him in the temple, and said to him, "See, you have been made well. Sin no more, lest a worse thing come upon you." The man departed and told the Jews that it was Jesus who had made him well."

John 8:3-11. "Then the scribes and Pharisees brought to Him a woman caught in adultery. And when they had set her in the midst, they said to Him, "Teacher, this woman was caught in adultery, in the very act. Now Moses, in the law, commanded us that such should be stoned. But what do You say?" This they said, testing Him, that they might have something of which to accuse Him. But Jesus stooped down and wrote on the ground with His finger, as though He did not hear. So when they continued asking Him, He raised Himself up and said to them, "He who is without sin among you, let him throw a stone at her first." And again He stooped down and wrote on the ground. Then those who heard it, being convicted by their conscience, went out one by one, beginning with the oldest even to the last. And Jesus was left alone, and the woman standing in the midst. When Jesus had raised Himself up and saw no one but the woman, He said to her, "Woman, where are those accusers of yours? Has no one condemned you?" She said, "No one, Lord." And Jesus said to her, "Neither do I condemn you; go and sin no more.""

What did the man who was healed in 5:1-15 and the woman brought to Jesus in 8:3-11 have in common?

Why was the woman not stoned?

What warning did Jesus give the healed man?

Take a Step of Faith

If you have not yet taken the step of faith, asked God for forgiveness and accepted Jesus Christ as your personal savior, please do not wait another moment. If you are ready, pray this simple prayer: *Lord, please forgive me of my sins. Wash me clean and make me new. I accept that Jesus died in my place. I accept the free gift of grace and forgiveness in Christ Jesus. Teach me and guide me in Your ways. In Jesus' name I pray, Amen.*

Whether or not you have taken the step of faith now or in the past, write down in a journal or notebook your questions to God and ask Him to reveal the answers to you. Realize that God answers prayers in His time. Pray for patience, faith and an open mind to receive God's answers to your prayers.

Do you ever wonder where you are in your faith journey? Below is a simple assessment that can help guide you in the areas where you are weak and/or strong. Ranging from 1 to 10 points, add your total at the bottom. Give yourself 1 point for each statement for *"I believe and I am certain"* up to 10 points for *"I do not believe."* For example, if you partially believe the statement, give yourself a "5" on it.

1. ____I believe that God is Holy and Righteous.

2. ____I believe that I am a sinner and in need of God's forgiveness.

3. ____I believe that I am saved.

4. ____I believe that I will be in God's Presence when I die.

____Total

Reflect on your answers to the questions that you just answered. How close are to you to the total number of 4? How close do you want to be? If you are left wondering about the depth of your faith, please ask God to enter into your life and reveal to you His will. Open your heart and mind to what He wants from you. Remember to let go of preconceived ideas and allow the Holy Spirit to speak directly to you. Be patient. God is not a vending machine. He wants your whole heart and mind. If your motives are pure and you sincerely seek His will, He will answer you in His time.

Read these verses on God's love for you:

Revelation 21:4. "And God will wipe away every tear from their eyes; there shall be no more death, nor sorrow, nor crying. There shall be no more pain, for the former things have passed away."

Deuteronomy 33:27. "The eternal God is your refuge, And underneath are the everlasting arms; He will thrust out the enemy from before you, And will say, 'Destroy.'"

Zephaniah 3:17. "The Lord your God in your midst, The Mighty One will save; He will rejoice over you with gladness, He will quiet you with His love, he will rejoice over you with singing."

The Ultimate Demonstration of Love- John 3:16-17

"For God so loved the world that He gave His only begotten Son, that whoever believes in Him should not perish but have everlasting life. For God did not send His Son into the world to condemn the world, but that the world through Him might be saved."

Lesson 8 - Love God Love Peoples

Jesus spoke ideas and truths that rocked the foundation of the beliefs of both Jews and gentiles. Threatened by this charismatic spiritual leader, some very powerful Jewish leaders wanted Jesus to be arrested and killed for his teachings. Comments considered blasphemous or denouncements of the Roman king warranted severe penalties. As the authorities sought to bait Jesus into making a punishable statement, both Matthew and Mark record the stories of how Jesus astonished people and silenced Sadducees with His answers. In one case, a man educated in the Jewish law asked Jesus, "Which is the greatest commandment of all?" First in Exodus and recounted in Deuteronomy, the story of Moses receiving the Ten Commandments from God is of great historical and spiritual importance to the Jewish people as it is for Christians and Jews today. As the original writer of the Commandments, Jesus brilliantly weaves all of the Ten Commandments into His answer: "Jesus said to him, 'You shall love the Lord your God with all your heart, with all your soul, and with all your mind.' This is the first and great commandment. And the second is like it: 'You shall love your neighbor as yourself.' On these two commandments hang all the Law and the Prophets" (Matthew 22:37-40).

The first five Commandments instruct us how we are to love God by putting Him first, not worshipping idols, not taking His name in vain, keeping the Sabbath day for God and by honoring our mother and father. These are the "Love God" Commandments. The second five Commandments instruct us how we are to love our neighbors by not lying to them, stealing from them, not sleeping with their spouses, not killing them and not envying what they have. These are the "Love Peoples" Commandments. In His answer, Jesus tells the listeners that they are to love their neighbors as themselves.

People who have strong bonds with family, spouses and friends usually understand the importance of and have an appreciation for the love that they share. Yet loving people who do not share our DNA, neighborhood, values, belief systems or political preferences is usually not a primary focus in our lives. If we are brutally honest with ourselves, we should acknowledge that we fail miserably to love our neighbors, let alone love our neighbors as ourselves. Why is there such a high bar set by Jesus? Some Bible scholars argue that this is at its core a lesson in grace. God wrote the law, yet He knew that the law was not achievable in our human weakness. It is to teach us how far we are from the perfection of the God who created us. It is only when we have that "ah-ha" realization of our lowliness and sinfulness that we understand that we need Jesus. God designed us to need Him. He put the entire plan in place so that we can be perfected in and through Christ. Without Christ, we are nothing and incapable of being "good enough" to earn our way to heaven. We are not and will never be good enough without the saving grace of the Lord Jesus Christ.

Although we will not literally achieve loving our neighbors as we are commanded, it is not an excuse to ignore God's law. When we truly commit to walking with the Lord, our hearts become more aligned with the heart of God. Where some may have a deep compassion for the homeless, others may have compassion for shut-in seniors or victims of abuse or disasters. It is through the giving of ourselves to our neighbors that we can find joy in obedience to God.

The Ten Commandments. Exodus 20:2-17.

1. You shall have no other gods before me.

2. You shall make no idols.

3. You shall not take the name of the Lord your God in vain.

4. Remember the Sabbath day, to keep it holy.

5. Honor your father and your mother.

6. You shall not murder.

7. You shall not commit adultery.

8. You shall not steal.

9. You shall not bear false witness against your neighbor.

10. You shall not covet.

Scriptures about loving one another:

1 Corinthians 13:4-8. "Love is patient, love is kind. It does not envy, it does not boast, it is not proud. It does not dishonor others, it is not self-seeking, it is not easily angered, it keeps no record of wrongs. Love does not delight in evil but rejoices with the truth. It always protects, always trusts, always hopes, always perseveres" (NIV).

It is not uncommon to hear this scripture at weddings even when the couples getting married are not followers of Jesus Christ. Not only does this scripture teach us about God's love for us but it calls on us to apply its truths with one another. Read 1 Corinthians 13:4-8 again and reflect on the beauty of the message.

Romans 13:10. "Love does no harm to a neighbor; therefore love is the fulfillment of the law."

Ephesians 4:2. "With all lowliness and gentleness, with long suffering, bearing with one another in love...."

1 Peter 4:8. "And above all things have fervent love for one another, for "love will cover a multitude of sins."

John 15:13. "Greater love has no one than this, than to lay down one's life for his friends."

John 13:34-35. "A new commandment I give to you, that you love one another: just as I have loved you, you also are to love one another. By this all people will know that you are my disciples, if you have love for one another."

Scriptures that instruct us to love our enemies:

Luke 6:35. "But love your enemies, do good, and lend, hoping for nothing in return; and your reward will be great, and you will be sons of the Most High. For He is kind to the unthankful and evil."

Matthew 5:44. "But I say to you, love your enemies, bless those who curse you, do good to those who hate you, and pray for those who spitefully use you and persecute you."

Proverbs 25:21-22. "If your enemy is hungry, give him bread to eat; And if he is thirsty, give him water to drink; For so you will heap coals of fire on his head, And the Lord will reward you."

Luke 6:28. "...bless those who curse you, and pray for those who spitefully use you."

Who are your neighbors?

What does it mean to you to love your enemies?

In Closing

Imagine that you are God and that you want a relationship with the people you have created. You give them a wonderful world to live in with all the resources they need to feed and house themselves. You give prophetic words to some of your people so that all people will believe in you when the prophecies come true. You give them a written instruction manual to tell them how to best live in peace and hope. You even enter into their world experience to teach them face-to-face about yourself, suffer a horrific death to cover the destructive effects of sin and appear in person to hundreds of people after your death so that your story can be shared for generations. Yet, it isn't enough for some people. Their hearts are hardened and many reject you. "God, who at various times and in various ways spoke in time past to the father by the prophets, has in these last days spoken to us by His Son, whom He has appointed heir of all things, through whom also He made the worlds" (Hebrews 1:1-2).

There are many reasons why people reject Jesus including the false teachings of men. There are over fifty passages in the scriptures that warn of false teachers including, "Watch out for false prophets. They come to you in sheep's clothing, but inwardly they are ferocious wolves" (Matthew 7:15). False teachers offer neither the depth of prophetic evidence as seen in the Bible nor compelling substantiation of a Messiah who rose from the grave.

The Christian faith is a journey and not a destination. Through Bible study, prayer, fellowship with other believers and faith, Christians dedicate themselves to becoming more and more like Jesus every day. It is through these actions that Christians develop a deep personal relationship with Him. A mature relationship with God is the key to peace and joy regardless of the circumstances this life throws our way. Nothing in the Bible tells us that life is easier for Christians, that we will have all of our prayers answered in the way that we desire or that we will not sin and fall short. Yet living in a Christ-centered way is the key to living a purposeful life. If you are already on this wonderful journey, may you love God and love Peoples more today than ever. Frustrations and disappointments will come and it is how we react to them that demonstrates our maturity. Think for a moment, how would your life change if the first thought when confronted with a challenge was, *What can I do right now to display love for God and love for people?* Doing what is in right in God's eyes rather than the push and pull of our innate selfishness can positively transform not only how others perceive you but how you perceive yourself. In the end, it is only how God perceives us and our hearts that really matters. If you died today, do you think you would hear from God, "Well done, good and faithful servant?" (Matthew 25:21)

I hope that this Bible study has challenged you to seriously consider your relationship with God, whatever stage it is in. There is so much more that I would love to share with you about God's love if you and I were having coffee (tea for me, please). Fortunately, the God of the Universe is as close to you as you want Him to be. He is a gentleman and is patiently waiting for you to open the door of your heart to Him.

May the God of the Universe richly bless you, protect you, and comfort you in your times of plenty and in your times of need. May His light shine upon you and may you reflect that light back into the world in praise of His love and His Glory. God bless you, my friend!

Works Cited

Brumbaugh, Robert S. and Wells, Rulon S. *The Yale University Library Gazette* Vol. 64, No. 1/2 (October 1989)

Comfort, Ray. *Scientific Facts in the Bible*, (Newberry, Fl: Bridge-Logos, 2001)

Comfort, Ray. *How to Know God Exists*, (Alachua, FL: Bridge-Logos, 2007)

Fales, Richard complied by Comfort, Ray. *"Archaeology and History attest to the Reliability of the Bible,"* in *The Evidence Bible*, (Bridge-Logos Publishers, Gainesville, FL, 2001)

Gleason, Dr., Archer. *A Survey of Old Testament Introduction*, (Chicago IL: Moody Publishers, 1974)

Hutchinson, Robert J. *The Politically Incorrect Guide to the Bible*, (Washington DC: Regnery Publishing, Inc. 2007)

Geisler, Norman & Bocchino, Peter. *Unshakeable Foundations,* (Minneapolis, MN: Bethany House Publishers, 2001)

Geisler, Norman and Nix, William. *A General Introduction to the Bible,* (Chicago IL, Moody Press, 1974)

Geisler, Norman and Brooks, Ronald. *When Skeptics Ask* (Wheaton, Illinois: Victor Books, 1990)

Wycliffe, *Why Bible Translation*, https://www.wycliffe.org/about/why Accessed 27 Sept. 2017.

www.ingramcontent.com/pod-product-compliance
Lightning Source LLC
Chambersburg PA
CBHW060617030426
42337CB00018B/3082